C000062494

IMAGES OF ENGLAND

BLYTH II

IMAGES OF ENGLAND

BLYTH II

BOB BALMER & GORDON SMITH

TEMPUS

Frontispiece: Thought to be the oldest known photograph of Blyth, this image shows the laying of the foundation stone for the new Wesleyan church in Waterloo on the 17 September 1867 by the Revd Robert Hayworth of Gateshead. The church was later known as the Central Methodist Church. The last service in the church was held on Easter Sunday on the 25 March 1989; the congregation then moved to a newly built church in Beaconsfield Street and the old building was demolished to make way for the Keel Row shopping mall. The area in the foreground which was tidal then is now where the present bus station is situated.

First published 2004

Tempus Publishing Limited
The Mill, Brimscombe Port,
Stroud, Gloucestershire, GL5 2QG
www.tempus-publishing.com

© Bob Balmer & Gordon Smith, 2004

The right of Bob Balmer & Gordon Smith to be identified as the Authors of this work has been asserted in accordance with the Copyrights, Designs and Patents Act 1988.

All rights reserved. No part of this book may be reprinted or reproduced or utilised in any form or by any electronic, mechanical or other means, now known or hereafter invented, including photocopying and recording, or in any information storage or retrieval system, without the permission in writing from the Publishers.

British Library Cataloguing in Publication Data.
A catalogue record for this book is available from the British Library.

ISBN 0 7524 3349 0
Typesetting and origination by Tempus Publishing Limited.
Printed in Great Britain.

Contents

Blyth Grammar School Sports Day in 1956. Two of the female competitors, Val Atkinson and Lil Richardson, were pictured with their friends, Alan Scott and Bob Newall.

Eileen Wade (with the brush) and a shop assistant clearing snow from the front of her shop in Havelock Street on 17 November 1969. The shops on the far side of Bridge Street were all demolished to make way for the Keel Row shopping mall.

Acknowledgements

Thanks must go to all those people, too numerous to mention by name, who over the years have contributed background information to many of the photographs used in this book. Thanks must also go to Ms Angela Johnstone for her encouragement and for proofreading the book. Acknowledgement is also given to the following for the use of photographs in this book: Blyth Local History Society, Blyth Local Studies Group, Blyth Harbour Commission, North East Press Ltd.

While every effort has been made to ensure the accuracy of the text, the Blyth Local Studies Group would like to hear from anyone who may have further information about photographs used in the book. If anyone has photographs of local interest which should be recorded, the Group would like to hear from you. Please contact:
Blyth Local Studies Group
c/o 95 Disraeli Street
Blyth NE24 1JB.

Introduction

Although Blyth's port dates back to the twelfth century, the town of Blyth is in fact quite modern, dating from the end of the first quarter of the eighteenth century. From this date until November 1900 this area was known as South Blyth; Blyth Pans, Blyth Quay and the hamlet of North Blyth were on the north side of the river. During the remainder of the eighteenth century the town of Blyth slowly started to take shape with the development of the land between Northumberland Street (now Bridge Street) and the river. Such streets as Bath Terrace, Caroline Street, Northumberland Street, Queens Lane, Tate Street, Ridley Street, Sea View, Sussex Street, the Wapping, the Quayside and Nelson Place were built. Caroline Street, named after Queen Caroline, was renamed Blagdon Street in the early nineteenth century and Northumberland Street was renamed Bridge Street in 1967. Bridge Street, formerly New Bridge Street, dates from after 1840 when the Waterloo Bridge was built, and Middleton's Yard seems to date from about 1850. With the main housing growth of the area taking place after 1850, any of the old buildings that still exist in the town from this date are of a plain and functional style typical of the Victorian working-class towns in the north-east of England.

The major developments in the area can be said to start from after the formation of the two local boards, South Blyth Local Board on 17 March 1863, and Cowpen Local Board on 18 April 1864. At this date the Cowpen Local Board only consisted of the two hamlets of Waterloo and Cowpen Quay. Both districts were later extended into the surrounding area and under the Local Government Act of 1894 became urban district councils. The South Blyth Urban District consisted of South Blyth and the hamlet of Crofton, with Newsham and New Delaval being added later. The Cowpen Urban District consisted of the hamlets of Waterloo, Cowpen Colliery, Cowpen Quay, Cowpen Square, (all now part of the town of Blyth) and the village of Cowpen with Bebside being added later. In 1907 the Blyth and Cowpen districts were amalgamated under one name to form the Blyth Urban District Council and on 28 August 1922, under Royal Charter, Blyth became as it is today, a municipal borough with its own Mayor.

The principal industries in the area have been coalmining, fishing, shipbuilding and, at one time, the salt trade – from the thirteenth century until the end of the eighteenth century. Coalmining in the Blyth area dates from about the end of the eleventh century when small Bell Pits were being worked by the monks from Newminster and Tynemouth priories. By the fifteenth century over 21,000 tons of coal were being shipped from the river Blyth. With the opening of deep mines at Cowpen Colliery in 1796 and at Cowpen Square in 1804 the yearly tonnage of coal shipped had reached 250,000 tons by 1855.

With the formation of the Blyth Harbour & Dock Co. in 1853 and the passing of the 1858 Harbour Act, which permitted dredging in the harbour, improvements in trade at the port began. The formation of the Blyth Harbour Commission in 1882 brought about major developments in the port, such as the building of new coal-loading staithes and the building of the Import Dock or the South Harbour as most locals know it. With larger collieries and better coal handling equipment, by the beginning of the twentieth century, over 3 million tons of coal were being shipped out of the port; by 1930 this had reached 5.5 million tons. Of the six pits at Blyth in the 1930s, only one was left by the early 1970s, and this closed after the miners strike in 1984. At the beginning of the twenty-first century there are no coal staithes left standing and the only coal to be shipped from Blyth is the odd cargo of coal from opencast mines.

Recorded shipbuilding at the port dates from 1740, but there was probably shipbuilding here a lot earlier than that. During the French Wars (1795–1815) there were five shipbuilding yards at the port, two at North Blyth and three at South Blyth; by the mid-nineteenth century only three small yards on the south side were still working. With the advent of iron, and then later steel vessels the layout of the yards became less in number but bigger in size. By 1925 there was only one yard, which stretched from the north end of the quayside up to the Golden Fleece, with six building berths and five dry docks. This all came to an end in 1966 when Blyth Dry Docks & Shipbuilding Co. Ltd announced it was closing down.

At the beginning of the twenty-first century the port is only a faint shadow of its former days; other industries have come and gone and Blyth is now only a part of the vast commuter belt serving North Tyneside and Newcastle.

Bob Balmer
Blyth Local Studies Group
June 2004

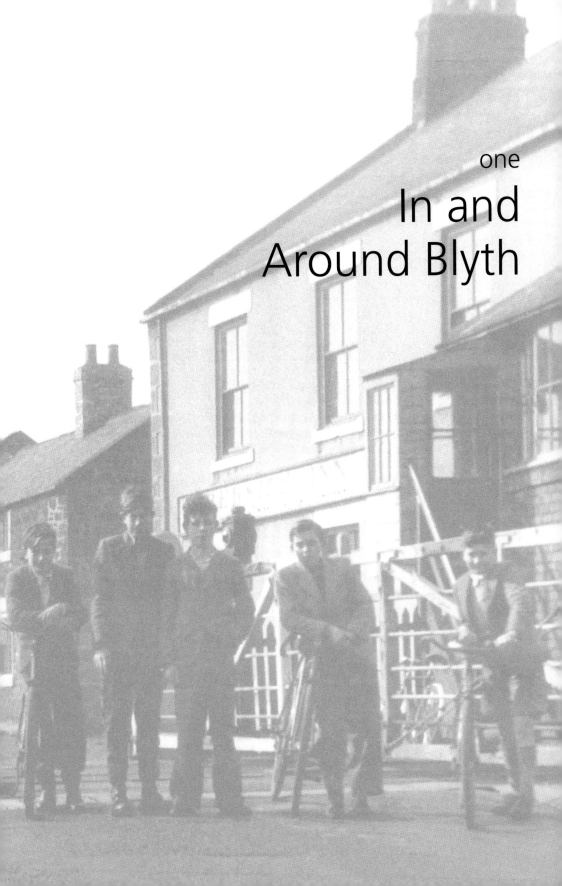

one

In and
Around Blyth

From the state of the unmade roadway this picture of Market Street must date from the late 1890s. Alder's were jewellers and compass adjusters. In the far distance is Blyth's post office, which was built in 1893.

Northumberland Street in the late 1890s. Note the sandstone houses on the left before St Cuthbert's churchyard; these houses were about 150 years old when they were demolished in the early 1900s to make way for the building of Wellington Street.

Blagdon Street in approximately 1900. It was formerly known as Caroline Street and is now Bridge Street. In 1900, Blagdon Street was one of the main shopping areas for Blyth. The shop on the left corner is George Swalwell's beehive store and the one on the right is Jacob Keenlyside's ship chandlers store. Jacob was the last man in Blyth to mount a whaling expedition to Southern Waters in the early twentieth century.

This old Georgian house at the southern end of Northumberland Street is referred to as the Old Vicarage, but it had been built and used for a lot longer as Lord Ridley's Estate Office. The building was demolished in the 1990s after standing for many years in a derelict condition.

The newly built Ridley Avenue in approximately 1920. Note the young trees lining the street; those trees today practically meet each other above the roadway. Not all the houses were built at the same time; it was a number of years before all the building plots were sold.

Looking east up Bridge Street just before the First World War with the Blyth & Tyne Brewery buildings visible above and behind the Brewery Bar. Note the old style steam roller laying a new road surface. One wonders if this was a Sunday as there were so few people about.

Looking down the north side of Bridge Street showing the original houses that were built in about 1850. Known then as New Bridge Street, some of the town doctors and vice-consuls lived in this road. The three-storey buildings further down the street were all built in the early 1900s.

Looking down the south side of Bridge Street, the earliest buildings here range from 1861 when the first of the shops on the left were built. The Presbyterian church was built in 1865, the Mechanics Institute, which is now the Library, was built in 1883 and Hedley & Young's was built in 1896.

Looking from Bridge Street towards the Market Place, on the right is the imposing front of the Central Methodist church. The fence to the right of it was where G. & N. Wright's timber yard stood; this area is now the bus station. The large building in the centre of the picture is the Central Hall, built in 1858; this building was destroyed by fire on 17 January 1923 and when it was rebuilt it opened as a cinema.

The east side of Blagdon Street before it was demolished during the second quarter of the twentieth century. In the 1850s there were seven shops on this side of the street but by 1890 there were only three: Swalwell's beehive store; Cuthbert Foster, the chemist; and John Hedley's large drapery and furniture store.

Looking west up Waterloo Road from the Market Place in approximately 1900, on the right is the Central Hall with the Zion Methodist church at the other end of the block. On the left are all the little shops that slowly disappeared over the years. The Blyth Co-op store was one of these; the building was expanded into the the present Northumbria House.

Turner Street, *c.* 1900. The gap in the street next to the Commercial Inn was known as Turner Square; this disappeared when Burton's, the tailors shop, was built in the early 1920s. The large shop on the corner of Market Street was the Cash Boot Co., which was first established there in 1893.

After eighteen hours of heavy rain and sleet the folks of Blyth awoke on the Saturday morning of 27 October 1900 to find the place awash. The flood finally started to subside on the Sunday afternoon and Blyth's new steam fire engine was brought into use pumping out the shops and the cellars of the public houses.

At the height of the flood the depth of the water in some of the houses in Folly Road (Park Road) reached the keyboards of their pianos in the front rooms. On the Sunday the milkman still had difficulties in doing his milk round in this part of the town.

Looking up Turner Street from the Market Place, *c.* 1910. On the left is Pius Kelly's the drapers, with the Salvation Army hall above and, near the corner, Shy the Butcher, Jones Sewing Machine shop and the Cash Boot Co. Note the baker's hand cart outside Marshall's the bakers on the right, and one of those noisy motor cars being chased down the middle of the road by a dog.

Looking down Turner Street with the railway station on the right, *c.* 1900. On the left is C. Pordum the hatter and outfitter followed by the Railway Hotel, which is now the Pullman; next was the Maypole Butter Co. store and J. W. Chisholm's large furniture showroom, which, along with Frank T. Wallace's drapery shop in Seaforth Street, were totally destroyed by fire on Wednesday 26 October 1904.

This view of the old council offices only existed for a short period before they were demolished in 1989. When Seaforth Street and Simpson Street were standing, the only part you could see was the central portion across the head of Seaforth Street.

Looking up Regent Street in approximately 1930 with the cranes of the Cowpen Shipbuilding & Dry Dock Co. in the background. The only buses that passed through Cowpen Quay had to be single-deckers because of the low and narrow railway bridge beside the railway station. The two tall buildings in the distance on the left are the Buffalo Hotel and Regent Street Methodist church.

Cowpen Square and the Ferry Corner in the mid-1930s. The whole of Cowpen Square is still standing but nearly all of Crofton Mills have been demolished. At this date the shipyard had not yet extended to the High Ferry but had encroached over Wimbourne Road, which ran from Regent Street to the riverside. The council houses in Crawford Street and Millfield Gardens had not long been built. In the bottom left corner is the Travellers Rest hotel and in the upper left corner is Factory Point and the local authority and Port Health isolation hospital.

Blyth's first hospital was two workmen's cottages given by Sir Matthew White Ridley to Dr Gilbert Ward in 1863. The site of the hospital was near the corner of the present Park View and Ridley Avenue. Over the years the hospital became known as Dr Ward's Hospital because of his great interest and work in it.

Dr Gilbert Ward Esq. MCSLH was a surgeon and medical officer for the Blyth district of Tynemouth Union, and was also a ship owner. He founded the Blyth Cottage Hospital and was the main driving force behind the formation of the Thomas Knight Memorial Hospital.

MASTER'S CERTIFICATE OF SERVICE.

(Issued pursuant to the Act 13th and 14th Vict., cap. 93.)

N°. 42.6/5 *Fifteen.*

Number Forty-Two Thousand Six Hundred and *Fifteen.*

Thomas Knight

Born at *Buckland* County of *Kent* on the *25 Dec 1806*
Has been employed in the Capacities of *App. Mate and Master 28* years in the British Merchant Service ~~principally~~ in *the Foreign & Coasting* Trade.

Bearer's Signature *Thomas Knight*

Granted by the REGISTRAR GENERAL OF SEAMEN, LONDON. By order of the BOARD OF TRADE.

M. Brown, Registrar.

Issued at *Blyth*
this *31st* day of *Dec.* 1850

. *Any Person Forging, Altering, or Fraudulently using this Certificate, will be subject to a penalty of* FIFTY POUNDS, *or* THREE MONTHS' *Imprisonment with or without* HARD LABOUR ; *and any other than the Person it belongs to becoming possessed of this Certificate, is required to transmit it forthwith to the* REGISTRAR GENERAL OF SEAMEN, LONDON.

No. OF REGISTER TICKET.

Thomas Knight, a self-made Blyth businessman and ship owner, died on 28 March 1878. When Margaret, his widow, died in April 1879 she left a legacy of £6,000 to endow a hospital for the sick and lame poor of South Blyth, Newsham and Cowpen. None of the money was to be used for a hospital building.

With the help of others, Dr Ward managed to raise £2,000 to build the hospital and John and William Simpson, of Blyth, were given the contract to build it. The Thomas Knight Memorial Hospital was opened on 28 December 1887. After becoming a nursing home in 1987, the old building was demolished in 2003.

John Goulding and his wife Mary, the Charter Mayor and Mayoress of Blyth. John was born at Blyth in the early 1860s and, like his father, became a master builder. He served on Blyth Council from 1896 to 1928 and was honoured with the role of Charter Mayor on 9 November 1922 when Blyth became a municipal borough.

Large crowds gathered in the Market Place and beside Hedley's Fountain on 9 November 1922 to hear the town clerk read the Royal Charter that had been granted on 21 September proclaiming Blyth a municipal corporation.

After the speeches in Waterloo Market Place on Charter Day, the civic dignitaries march away with Cowpen Colliery Band at the head, followed by a guard of honour of firemen from the Blyth council fire brigade.

Cowpen Hall, *c.* 1950. Warburton described the hall (*c.* 1715) as 'a handsome seat, built with red brick'. Cowpen Hall was the ancestral seat of the Sidney family for many generations until the first quarter of the twentieth century. The old hall had many uses before it was demolished in 1958. The Cowpen & Bebside British Legion social club was built on the site.

Cowpen village, *c.* 1910. On the left is the Windmill Inn and on the right the Co-operative store and what looks like road-surfacing work going on in the distance. If a photographer tried to take a picture from the same spot on Cowpen Road today he would be putting his life in danger.

This picture shows the road works in progress beside St Cuthbert's church in Cowpen during July 1968. Part of the churchyard at each side of the road was removed to widen and straighten the road.

Looking west along Cowpen Lane, Kitty Brewster stands beside the Percy Arms, *c.* 1900. Most of the buildings in this picture were demolished under the Slum Clearance Acts of the early 1930s to make way for modern council housing, which was built in 1938.

Looking east down Cowpen Lane towards Cowpen village, *c.* 1900. This tranquil rural scene with the cows slowly strolling down the middle of the road as they make their way towards the farm is a far cry from what Cowpen Road is nowadays. In the 1960s the roadway through Cowpen and Kitty Brewster was straightened and widened to take modern traffic.

Above: Road work for the Kitty Brewster bridge had started before the Second World War but work on the bridge itself was delayed until after the war, and because of steel shortages, it was not until February 1960 that the steel work for the bridge was fully underway.

Left: The first of the two huge steel trestles to support the Kitty Brewster road bridge was completed on 16 August 1960. All the steel work for the bridge was made by the Blyth Dry Docks & Shipbuilding Co., and most of it was transported to the bridge by road.

The first of four 130ft long steel girders leaves Blyth shipyard on 18 August 1960. Minutes after this photograph was taken it slipped off the trailer and blocked Hodgsons Road. It finally reached the bridge site hours late. Because of this the other three girders were floated one at a time up the river to the bridge on a specially built raft.

Alderman Nicholas Garrow (left), Alderman Dan Dawson and Mr Alec Cheyne begin their walk over the new Kitty Brewster road bridge just seconds after Alderman Dawson, the Chairman of the County Highways Committee, had cut the ceremonial tape on Saturday 15 April 1961.

A group of Bebside lads stop to have their photograph taken with the north side of Front Street, Bebside, in the background, *c.* 1952. The lads left to right are Henry Hedley, Ralph Johnson, Raymond Maughan, Ralph Race and Jimmy Orr.

Front Street, Bebside, looking towards the railway crossing, *c.* 1890. Although the colliery village has gas lights in the street, the paths and main road look to be just plain earth, which in winter and during wet periods must have led to a lot of dirt being carried into the houses on people's feet. The colliery houses were plain stone-built houses, and were well known in the area for their white-painted door and window surrounds and black-painted doors and window shutters.

Front Street, Bebside, in about 1920. Although the roadway still looks a bit rough, the footpaths have been made up and there is a march of telegraph poles through the village. By this date there was a bus service between Blyth and Bebside and another hourly service from Blyth to Ashington, via the Furnace Bank.

Looking down the rear of Front Street, Bebside, *c.* 1950. The colliery houses were built of rough sandstone and originally consisted of two rooms upstairs and two rooms downstairs. The stone offshoots at the back of the houses were added long after the street had been built and were used as the kitchen. For many years there was no plumbing in the houses; there was a water tap opposite every twelfth house for the use of the whole street. People had to cross the back lane to go to the toilet.

Bebside Hall was probably built with stone from the old Hall, which dated from the twelfth century and was demolished during the Reformation, in the late sixteenth century or early seventeenth century. The old hall was situated on the north side of the Bebside to Horton Road. The big house and farm buildings on this site were demolished in May 2004.

Newsham North Farm, built in 1886, stands on the site of an old mansion house that had been built in 1561. Wallace (c. 1858) states: 'This mansion is still standing, and has long been occupied as a farmhouse by the Wilson family. It presents a fine example of the dwellings of the lesser gentry of 300 years ago.' Members of the Wilson family still live in the farm today.

The newly built Cowpen & Bebside British Legion social club was built on the site of Cowpen Hall in 1958-59. In its heyday it was a hive of entertainment but like so many other clubs it felt the pinch of dropping members. This building was demolished in 1999.

This building is on the site of the old Cowpen Colliery Inn that opened in the mid-1850s. George Hudson is given as the first licence holder and his occupation is listed as 'Beer House Keeper & Shepherd'. The present building dates from 1900 when it was built as the Cowpen Colliery Hotel. Throughout most of its life this pub has always been known as The Top House. And so it is now called.

The original Buffalo Inn at Keelmans Row later became part of Regent Street in Cowpen Quay. John Crawford held the licence from 2 January 1890 until May 1897. The first mention of the Inn is in an 1841 Trade Directory when Lionel Aynsley held the licence.

The bar staff at the Buffalo Hotel in Cowpen Quay, *c.* 1910. During 1899 the old Buffalo Inn was demolished and a much larger Buffalo Hotel was built. The public house finally closed in July 1975 but the building is still in use today as a community centre.

This building was formerly called the Brown Cow Inn but by 1822 it was being called the Dun Cow Inn. The above was built in the 1880s when the Dun Cow Hotel was built. John Northover held the licence between 1822 and 1834. The building was damaged by fire in December 1976 and was finally demolished in December 1987 after being used, at one point, as a fishing-tackle shop.

The first pub called The Golden Fleece seems to date from 1870. For many years it was the headquarters for rowing events on the river with its own boathouse and boats. The present building was opened in May 1881 after the old pub was destroyed by fire.

Robert Cooper Jnr was the landlord of the Globe Hotel in Waterloo Road from July 1892 until July 1901. Listed in 1834, the public house closed at Christmas 1978 and was converted into a branch of Hinton's supermarket in 1980.

The Windmill Inn in Cowpen village was built in 1905 to replace the old inn, which is the white cottage on the right of this picture. The old Windmill Inn is first mentioned in directories in 1825, with George Bell as the innkeeper, but may well be a lot older than that. From March 1905 until July 1920 the landlord of the Windmill Inn was George Adie.

two

Shops

Northumberland Street in the late 1890s. The shops at the top of the street were George Swalwell's beehive store and next door but one was M. Taylor's the grocer, tea and flour dealer. George Davis' little grocers shop on the right became a general dealers store owned by John T. Portious not long after this date.

Time Signal direct from Greenwich Daily.

Tel. No. 49.

Alder & Company,

B. N. I. T. A.

Nautical Instrument Makers and Compass Adjusters to Board of Trade and Norwegian Merchant Service.

Stationers and Chart Agents.

— Charts for all parts of the World. —

Repairs to Lamps, Logs, Steam & Vacuum Gauges promptly and Carefully Executed.

Ridley Street, (Opposite Quayside) Blyth.

A 1930 advertisement for Alder & Co.

Hedley & Young's Albion House built in 1896. It is interesting to note that before anything was built on this block of land from Bridge Street to Carlton Street, plans to build the new railway station here in the town centre were made, but the Thomas Knight Memorial Hospital objected to it on the grounds of noise

Above Left: Fashion shows were a regular thing at Hedley & Young's shop. Here we see Mavis Scott showing the latest fur coats in October 1964. A few years later Mavis Scott opened the Hat Box, a small milliner's shop on Regent Street.

Above Right: George Soulsby's butchers shop on the corner of the Central Hall and Waterloo Road with the Gospel Hall above, *c.* 1920. When the Central Hall was destroyed by fire on 17 January 1923 it was rebuilt as the cinema; on this corner was Martins Bank.

R.H. Maughan & Co., plumbers and gas fitters, started business in this shop on the corner of Sussex Street and Market Street (now Plessey Road) in 1896. By the end of the following year the business was being run by George Maughan who ran the company until the mid-1920s when it closed down. This shop is still there today, unchanged in appearance.

R. Thirlwell, the butcher, moved from Crofton into this shop on the corner of Alexandra Crescent (now Cowpen Road) and Harper Street in 1902 where he was in business for about ten years. The property then passed into the hands of James Young, the painters and decorators. Mrs Young also had a counter in the shop for the sale of sweets. They went out of business in the 1920s.

The Hard Hit Middle Classes

The Single-handed Housewife

Many are the housewives who are to-day compelled to do their own housework. Economy is a necessity for most, a duty for all domestic assistance is not easily secured.

Unless the housewife is to be deprived of all her leisure; and time for social and other occupations, her home must be truly up-to-date and fitted with modern, scientific, labour-saving appliances. Otherwise her day will be one of drudgery and weariness Any appliances which will help to lighten her load are to be welcomed.

Nothing simplifies domestic work so much as gas apparatus, clean, convenient, and cheap; the gas cooker, the gas refuse destructor, the gas fire, the gas water heater, and the gas washing copper are all undoubtedly improvements of a lasting value,

THE RIGHT KIND OF HOUSE.

Healthy Fires. Plentiful Hot Water. Modern Methods in the Kitchen

For further particulars apply to The

Blyth Gas Co., Bridge Street, Blyth

69

A 1930 advertisement for the Blyth Gas Co. in Bridge Street.

The first shop owned by Herron's, the watch and clock makers in Croft Street (now King Street) in Cowpen Quay. They started in business in 1841 and their shop was situated next door to the Fox and Hounds Inn, which they also owned. In about 1900 the business moved into a new shop in Regent Street from where they still work today.

Thomas Hunter, the watch maker, moved into a shop in Waterloo Road in 1897. He did not have good luck in these premises as his shop was flooded in October 1900 and then destroyed by fire in October 1904 yet he was still here in 1908. He then moved to Union Street where he was still trading in the 1920s.

Jacob Cooknell in the doorway of his drapery shop on the corner of Regent Street and Beaumont Street in Cowpen Quay, *c.* 1900. Jacob developed a Worsted and Stocking Knitting business at Blyth in the 1890s. He later purchased the Gaiety Theatre in Quay Road in Blyth, after it had been damaged by fire, to convert into a big manufacturing business.

Father and son, George Smith and George 'Pie' Smith Jnr (in the apron), in the doorway of their bakers and confectioners shop on the opposite side of Beaumont Street to Cooknell's shop, *c.* 1900. George 'Pie' Smith was the Blyth Carnival Queen (a role always played by a man) in 1929 and 1930.

Thomas and Septimus Mole's cycle works at Cowpen Quay, *c.* 1900. Both men were keen cyclists from about the 1880s. By the 1890s, Thomas was manufacturing bicycles at his Cowpen Quay works where he was joined by his brother in 1901. By 1908 Septimus had opened a bicycle shop on the front of the Central Hall in Waterloo. Just before the First World War Thomas moved his business into a shop in Regent Street.

John Blyth and his son standing in the doorway of his shop in Croft Road, *c.* 1898. In the late 1880s he had a shop at Cowpen Quay and moved into this shop in about 1890 where he remained in business until 1900. His son, also called John, was killed in action in France on Tuesday 3 September 1918.

Like many towns and mining villages in the North East, Bebside had its own Industrial Co-operative Society. This 1920s picture shows the whole of the staff, seventeen in all, from the manager down to the cobbler boy. This seems like a large number of staff but it must be remembered that a lot of the foodstuff came in bulk and then had to be weighed and bagged in the back shop; there were no pre-packed items in those days.

John Soulsby Jnr standing in the doorway of his butchers shop at the Market Place, *c.* 1890. Born in 1862 at Cowpen Quay, the son of John Soulsby the shipwright, he served his apprenticeship with one of his uncles who also had butchers shops at Blyth and Cowpen Quay.

The Shy family have been butchers in the Blyth area since the mid-1870s. George Shy was born George Kraaft in Kunzelsau in Germany. The family lived at Goole in Yorkshire before moving to Blyth. Alfred Hall Shy had this shop on the corner of Market Street and Church Street for about thirty years from 1946.

Mrs Wilson standing in the doorway of her husband's fishmongers shop in Regent Street in Cowpen Quay, *c.* 1929. The shop closed on the outbreak of the Second World War and never reopened again.

A. Smithson, the painter and decorator, and glaziers shop on the corner of Simpson Street and Turner Street in Waterloo. This picture shows the shop decorated for the coronation of King George VI on Tuesday 12 May 1936.

Jean Fraser (the taller of the two) standing in the doorway of her shop in Waterloo Road with Connie Johnson beside her. As was the practice throughout the 1930s, the shop is decorated for Carnival Day to see if it could win a prize for the best-decorated small shop.

William Horn was born in 1826 at Ford near the Scottish border. He started working as a cobbler at Nelson Place in Blyth during the 1870s after serving his apprenticeship at Amble. By the early twentieth century he had become one of the leading evangelists, along with Colvin and Keenlyside, as can be seen from the front of his cobblers shop.

George R. Armstrong standing outside his shop on the corner of Station Street and Regent Street in Cowpen Quay with three of his staff in the mid-1930s. This shop won prizes a number of times during the Carnivals for being the best-decorated fruit shop.

The staff of the London & Newcastle Tea Co. shop on Waterloo Road, *c.* 1910. These new buildings and shops and the alleyway through to Croft Road were built after the fire on 16 October 1904. The little lad on the left looks like he has just left school. This shop is Boots, the chemists nowadays.

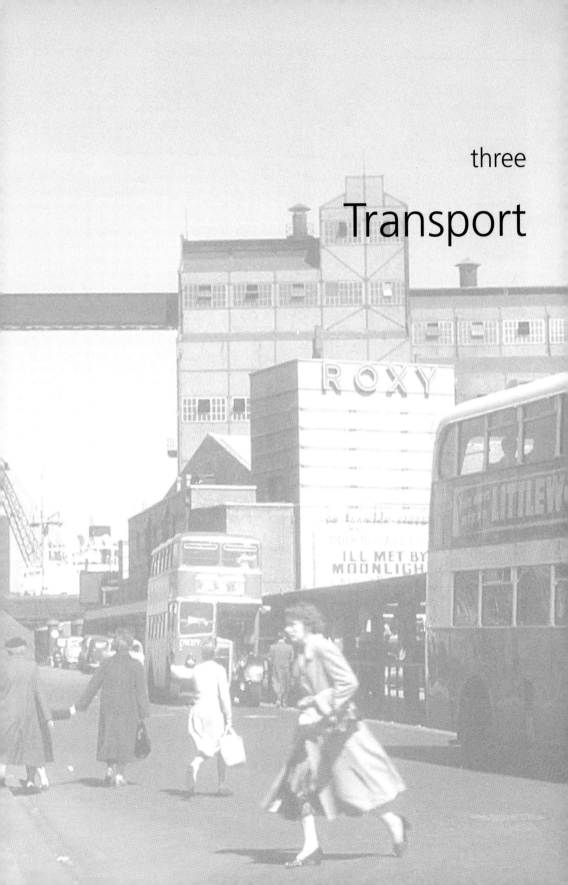

three

Transport

Hang on to your hats for a trip out into the countryside in a charabanc 1920s style. As the road surface looks more like a farm track, it makes it look like this may have been a bit of a bumpy ride. In bad weather the folding hood at the back came up over the passengers to keep them dry.

The United Automobile Services was registered as a company at Lowestoft in April 1912; by 1919 they had opened depots at Blyth and Ashington. This picture shows some of the fleet outside their garage in Wensleydale Terrace in 1921. The buses are all war surplus AEC chassis with a bus body added. The double-deckers were only single-deck bodies with a platform fitted on top and open to the weather.

By June 1921 Service 4 was well established, running via Newsham, High Pit, Seaton Burn and Gosforth. This service always had to be a single-decker because of the low arch under the railway at Dudley.

Thomas Allen, for many years a cab proprietor and owner of the livery stables, was running bus services between Blyth and Morpeth, Whitley Bay and Newcastle, and Newcastle and Ashington by 1923. As Blyth Motor Services, he ran a long-distance service between Newcastle and Aberdeen until the routes were bought out by United in 1934.

By October 1926, United was running a bus service to Cambois from Ashington. The bus in this picture was built as a single-decker with the upper deck added later; note the high step at the back to get onto the bus. The bus is in United's cream and brown livery, which was in use between 1923 and 1933. At this date there was no Highway Code to worry about – as you can see, he is on the wrong side of the road.

Blyth bus station in the late 1920s. This looks like a special trip, possibly to a football match at Newcastle, as it seems to be all men waiting to get on the buses. At this period Crate Bros of Blyth ran a service between Blyth and New Delaval and for a time, longer routes to Newcastle and Whitley Bay. These services were taken over by United in 1933 as were the services run by A.R. Douglas of New Delaval who ran buses between Blyth, New Delaval and New Hartley.

Blyth bus station during the 1930s. A. Howe of Blyth ('Pride of Blyth'), ran services between Blyth and North Shields and between Whitley Bay and North Shields via Marine Avenue. These services were bought by Tynemouth & District with United having a share of the Blyth to Whitley Bay section in 1934.

Blyth bus station in the 1940s. There was still very little shelter for people waiting for a bus. At one time, this area was called Town Hall Square as it was the proposed site for a new town hall; later it was renamed Post Office Square. It has always been known by locals as Blyth bus station.

Blyth bus station, *c.* 1959. Mrs Patterson in the foreground seems to be in a hurry. This picture shows
T. & B. Garage to the left and Roxy Cinema showing *Ill Met By Moonlight* to the right, with the gas works
behind it. Beyond that there is a large cargo vessel in No.3 dry dock waiting for repairs.

Two Blyth conductresses modelling United
Bus Co.'s new winter and summer uniforms
beside the United Garage in Plessey Road,
c. 1960. The hat did not go down too well
with the staff; it only seems to have lasted
about six months then it disappeared. The
conductress standing with one foot on the
step is Maureen Percival.

The large United bus garage on Plessey Road with Croft Park football ground behind it. This garage was built in the 1930s when the bus fleet became too large for the Wensleydale garage. At the height of its use there were about fifty buses based here; with the introduction of mini-buses this garage was closed in 1975 when a new smaller garage was built near the bus station.

South Blyth loco sheds were first built in 1879. They were enlarged to a six-track shed in 1895. Mainly housing locos for the mineral traffic to the staithes, the sheds finally closed on 27 May 1967. Although the site stood derelict for many years it is now covered by Blyth Community Hospital.

The interior of South Blyth loco sheds. When passenger traffic came to an end in 1964 the main traffic for the Blyth locomotives was hauling coal from the collieries of south-east Northumberland to either Blyth or the Tyne for shipment abroad.

A former Blyth & Tyne Railway 2-4-0 locomotive, class 21, No. 680 in North Eastern Railway livery at the old Blyth station, *c.* 1870. This old station was situated in Croft Street, now King Street, opposite the old Fox and Hounds Inn.

During the first half of 1850 the Bedlington Coal Co. built a railway across River Blyth on a huge wooden viaduct, which was 80ft high and 770ft long, to join their line to the Blyth to Percy main railway at Newsham. The Bedlington to Newsham line was opened to passenger traffic on 3 August 1850 and Cowpen Lane station was completed on 28 November 1850.

With the sinking of Bebside Pit in 1855 and the growth of the colliery village in Cowpen Lane, the station was renamed Bebside station in around 1862. In the early 1870s the platform was greatly lengthened but the accommodation was not, which brought about the remarks 'waiting room for fifty – platform for 500'. The building on the left of the crossing gates is the Bebside Inn and on the right of the gates is the station master's house.

'Newsham all change, Newsham all change' would be heard whenever a Blyth train pulled in to Newsham station. This picture of Newsham's ticket office, taken in approximately 1945, shows that you could get a ticket at one window for Newbiggin or Morpeth and the north, and at the other window for Newcastle and the south via Tynemouth and Jesmond.

A light train passing through the southern end of Newsham station on the down line. This picture shows the junction for the coal and passenger traffic to come to Blyth station and the coaling staithes at the quayside. On the left-hand side is part of the underpass that came out onto Carlton Avenue.

A tank loco with three carriages waiting at Newsham station before moving off for Blyth. Some wit suggested the driver and fireman were looking at a map to find out where they are. It is more than likely they are looking at the *Journal* to see what to put a bet on when they get back to Blyth.

With the growth of goods and passenger traffic Blyth station was rebuilt in 1895 on the site where Safeway now stands, most of the work being carried out by J.W. Simpson of Blyth at a cost of £20,000. This picture taken in approximately 1900 shows the station frontage and the entrance into the goods yard on the left.

Platform 1 of Blyth station in 1963. Although Blyth had only one long island platform with trains on each side, it numbered seven platforms. The raised portion on the left is where the coal lines passed the station to cross over the road bridge then on to the staithes on the quayside. It is now the raised part of Safeway's car park.

Platform 4 in 1963. Looking west down the platform with the goods yard on the left and the goods shed in the distance. The push/pull tank locomotive standing under the water point is standing at Platform 4.

Platform 5 in 1963. Looking back towards the station from the end of Platform 5 with the gasworks in the background and the goods shed on the right. As could be expected from the neatness of the shrubs and bushes, Blyth won prizes for being a tidy station.

A Stephenson Locomotive Society special, standing at the end of Platform 5 while on its North Eastern Tour in 1963. This area of the station was badly damaged when a mine exploded near the signal box, killing signalman Norfolk at 10.30 p.m. on Friday 25 April 1941.

Blyth Crossing at Cowpen Road in 1963. The western end of the loco sheds can be seen on the right. Behind the signal cabin is an old wartime static water tank that was constructed from 4ft square panels.

The pupils of Blyth Boys' Board School with Mr J. Jackson (seen with the beard) and two of his assistants in the 1890s. Locally the school was sometimes referred to as the Day School or Jackson's Academy. The school was situated in the Congregational Church school room in Carlton Street in Blyth. Mr Jackson was head of the school for about twenty-five years from the 1870s until it closed in the early 1900s.

Pupils at Snuffy Temple's School, c. 1881. From left to right, in the front row, are: ? Reed, ? Sutherland, ? Wood, ? Redford, Hugh Reid, Herbert Elgey and Foster Young. In the second row are: Hannah Rump, Bob Wilson, Dave Wood, Tom Young, Joe Sharp, Tom Thompson and Snuffy Temple. In the third row are: Bob Blackburn, Fred Wood, Billy Wilson, Billy Todd, Walter Best, Tom Craggs, Fred Temple (Snuffy's grandson) and Ned Dodds. In the back row are: J. Winter, Herbert Driver, Oswald Robinson, A. Blackburn, Robert Scott, Ralph Robinson, Billy Bell and Billy Brown.

Edward (Snuffy) Temple's School, *c.* 1881. The school was situated on the upper floor of a large square building at Crofton. Pupils paid 7s 6d a quarter, or 7 ½ d a week to attend the school. They had to buy their own textbooks and copybooks and Snuffy sold pen nibs at two a penny – only the ink was provided free. He retired in 1891 after upwards of sixty years as a teacher.

Blyth National School, *c.* 1890. A National School was opened in Wanley /Bowes Street in the same block as St Mary's church in 1858. Mr John Wallace was the teacher in charge and we are led to understand that he was a very strict disciplinarian.

Morpeth Road School, Class 7 in the early 1950s. Morpeth Road School opened in 1910 and Cowpen Colliery School closed with a number of the children coming to Morpeth Road School. Like a number of other schools in the Blyth area during the early years of the First World War, the children were moved out and troops moved in while they were based at Blyth for their training.

Plessey Road School, Group 7, c. 1919. Plessey Road School opened in 1892. At this date, an education still had to be paid for. During 1893, education became free for Infants and Standard 1. Earlier attempts to make some Blyth schools free had been resisted as it was felt unwise to establish 'pauper' schools.

New Delaval Infants School was built by the Seaton Delaval Coal Co., the local colliery owners, in 1874. The picture shows the girls at this school in 1887. Note the hand pump on the right-hand side that probably would have been the school's only supply of fresh water for many years.

Newsham School, built at a cost of £3,200, was opened during November 1876. It had accommodation for 516 pupils with one certificated teacher, one pupil teacher and a paid monitor.

Newsham Infants' School, Class IV in 1920. During the 1921 miners strike the feeding of 'necessitous school children' began and 236 children from Newsham were supplied with dinner at New Delaval's pavilion.

Blyth Grammar School in May 1956, Class 3 South. From left to right in the back row are: Bill Robson, Brian McCullock, Bob Newall, John Lynn, Wilson Smeaton, Desmond Rutherford, Fred Joicey and Les Hakin. In the middle row: ?, Maureen Irving, Pam Cummings, Anne Soulsby, Gordon Smith, Dudley Harcombe, Don Brydon, Anne Hanns, ? and Ros Baxter. In the front row: Margaret Frost, Mavis Hyde, Pat Lord, Eileen Mould, Mrs Swinney, Mary Foster, Kathleen Healey, Mildred Holloway and Evelyn Tait.

Blyth Grammar School Sports Day in 1956. Syb Woodman and Anne Hanns were competition winners for Ridley House.

Sixth formers in the chemistry laboratory at Blyth Grammar School in 1959.

In this photograph of Blyth Secondary School in Plessey Road, girls are doing physical training in the assembly hall and gym in approximately 1922. This school opened in 1913 when pupils transferred from the Higher Grade School in Beaconsfield Street with their headmaster Mr Gibbons. Boys and girls were educated separately until the death of the headmistress Miss Murdoch in 1932. It then became one school under the leadership of Mr N.O. Parry.

Wright Street School opened in 1876 as the first government-controlled school built in the Blyth area under the Local School Board, and for many years it was known as the 'Old Board School'. This picture shows the infants' class, *c.* 1910.

Wright Street School just after it closed in 1972. The building was taken over and run as Blyth Town Boys Club by the very well-known Jack Allen in 1977. The Boys Club had previously been held in the old cramped Irish Club across the street since 1946. By the 1990s, like many other youth clubs, it had to close for lack of members and by the beginning of the twenty-first century the old building was demolished.

five

Sport and Leisure

Left: At the time the most popular boxer throughout East Northumberland was Billy Johnson of Blyth who fought under the *nom-de-guerre* of Tiger Smith. He won the goodwill and appreciation of the boxing public during the late 1920s and early 1930s. He fought at Blyth, Ashington, Sunderland, St James' Hall in Newcastle, North Shields, South Shields and West Stanley. At his weight (8st 4lbs) he met some of the best men in the Northern Counties, a fair number of which he beat once and some of them twice. After his fighting days he worked at the Crofton Mill Pit in Crofton in Blyth.

Below: A. Rudd of Newsham Boys Club leads with a left to the face of G. Rutherford of Grainger Park Boys Club during the boxing contest on 6 April 1961 at the Cowpen and Crofton Welfare Hall in Blyth. The contest was held in aid of the Newsham Boys Club Building Fund.

Newsham Boys Club winners of the 1962 Northumberland County Association of Boys Clubs boxing championships. The following from left to right were the team, front row: A. Rudd, P. Hanlon and G. Brownles. Back row: Mr Alec Clifton (Trainer), D. Evans, M. Johnson, D. McNeal and Police Inspector G. McLanachan (the Club Chairman).

Blyth Cricket Club's 1925 cup winners. From left to right, front row: Smith, Bell, Beattie, Spence and Gallon. Back row: Bateley, Rooks, Coulthard, Batty, McLaughlin and Fletcher.

Blyth cricketers Peter Robertson and Graham Heatley. During the five seasons, 1963 to 1967, Peter Robertson took a total of 133 wickets for Blyth in Division A of the Northumberland League. Graham Heatley was another Blyth bowler who held the record twice for taking 10 wickets in a match, once in 1959 when he took 10-23 in 17.1 overs, and again in 1961 when he took 10-40 in 11.5 overs.

Blyth Spartans 1902/03. From left to right in the back row are: J. Purdy, D. Maltman, G. Robertson, F. Southern, J. Cannon, F. Frazer and R. Bird. Middle row: J. Archbold, E. Mount, D. Liddell, J. Evens, W. Harney and B. Rowell. Front row: H. Stenhouse, J. Baxter, R. Patton, P. McGlade and J. Archbold.

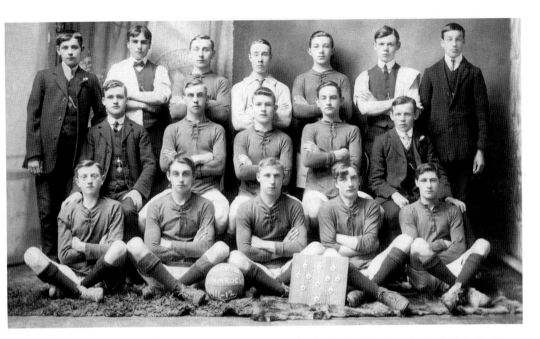

Blyth Shamrock 1911/12. The first Blyth team to reach the final of the Northumberland FA Junior Cup. From left to right in the front row are: Greener Miller, Bob 'Napper' Thompson, Dick Summerbell, Ted Ward and George Allen. Middle row: Bob Thompson (secretary), Jack Dodds, Fred Hanson, Tom Lillie, George Hogg (treasurer). Back row: Andre Yorke (reserve), George Wilkinson (trainer) Albert Telford, Arthur Howes, Wilf Mordue, John Bower (trainer) and Howard Irwin (committee).

Blyth Grammar School junior football team. From left to right, front row: R.D.H. Boyd (reserve). Seated: W.R. Dixon, D. Crosby, D. Chicken, J. Chicken and G.W. Robinson. Back row: A. Allonby, A. Wedderburn, Mr W.N. Linklater (master), D. Pearson, Mr W. Hall (master), W. Stoker, and A. Tate. They were the winners of the Blyth Secondary School's Junior League 1931/32 season.

Above: Bebside Secondary School senior girls netball team and winners of the George Cox Netball Shield in March 1964. From left to right, front row: Hilda Hall, Cynthia Holdsworth, Janet Davis (Capt) and June Douglas. Back row: Pauline Lesiol, Pauline McGowan, Miss M. Gallan (in charge of the team), Gloria Marshall and Irene Lesiol.

Left: Dr Ian Morton MacLachlan, born at Wooler, came to Blyth when he was very young. Always a keen sportsman, he played football with Blyth Spartans in the early 1920s and later played for Newcastle United as an amateur. He was also a handy cricketer, often holder of the Blyth Cricket Club's Tynemouth Senior League (Division A) batting and bowling averages. When he became a medical officer at Blackburn he played cricket in the Lancashire League.

The following are the team who competed in the Blyth rugby trials match on Saturday 21 October 1961 at the Cowpen Estate Ground. From left to right, front row: R. Gerner and L. Barron. Centre row: R. Langman, R. Whitlock, I. Wallace, J. Stevens and J. McLeod. Back row: B. Gallon, J. Bridon, J. Ward, G. Heatley, P. Conn, E. Abbel, J. Shaw and E. Potter.

E. Potter with the ball making the effort by which he scored a try for Blyth 'A' team on Saturday 24 February 1962 when they won 10-0 at home against Vickers III.

Members of Blyth Shipyard Cycling Club out on a club run. It is believed that this group photograph was taken near Mitford in Morpeth in the early 1930s. During the 1920s and 1930s there were at least three cycling clubs in Blyth: the above club, the Blyth & District Cycling Club and the Blyth Eagles.

The Fresh Air Fund was for Blyth children whose fathers were out of work. During the mid-1930s, day trips took children out into the countryside to places such as Alnwick, Rothbury and Hexham. They would later return to the grounds of Blagdon Hall on fine days or to Stannington Village Hall on wet days where each child was given a packed tea and a mug with the title and year of the trip upon it.

Blyth Grammar School Cadets, members of the Northumberland Army Cadet Force, having their annual inspection by a visiting officer in the 1950s.

Some of the youngsters in C Co. of the 2nd Northumberland Army Cadet Battalion stationed at Blyth in the Drill Hall on the Quayside along with the 272 Field Regiment Royal Artillery TA. Here some of the cadets are receiving sighting instruction on the Mark IV Lee Enfield .303 rifle from Capt Robert Aldcroft, CO of the Company.

The play area near the cafe at Blyth beach during a Bank Holiday in the 1950s. This picture was taken in the afternoon. As the day wore on and a cool breeze came in off the sea, the people would move off the beach to the other side of the sand dunes where it was sheltered and the children could play well into the early evening.

Blyth beach beside the promenade in the 1930s. The square green canvas tents were 6d a day to hire from the council attendant and the deck chairs were 3d to hire. A pot of boiling water to make tea could be bought for 1d at the Jubilee Cafe. On summer nights people would take their deck chair to the bandstand in the Beach Gardens and listen to music from a military band, a local colliery band or other musicians.

six

Port, Pit
and People

The East Pier Lighthouse was opened on Thursday 18 July 1907 by Mr John Whitfield. The lighthouse is equipped with a lantern of 60,000 candle power that gives a white group flashing light every 10 seconds, which is visible 15–20 miles out to sea. The pier end was a favourite place with the anglers but now you cannot get along the pier because of the group of windmills that have been built on the pier.

Work in progress in lengthening and encasing the old stone pier in concrete. This 1906 picture also shows the construction of the round end for the East Pier Light.

This early 1907 picture shows work in progress on the construction of the lighthouse at the end of the East Pier.

A view of the harbour entrance in approximately 1907 showing the South Harbour in its early stages of development before the present West Pier was constructed. On the right-hand side you have the old Ballast Jetty with the two steam cranes, one for removing the ballast from ships, the other to load it into wagons to take it away.

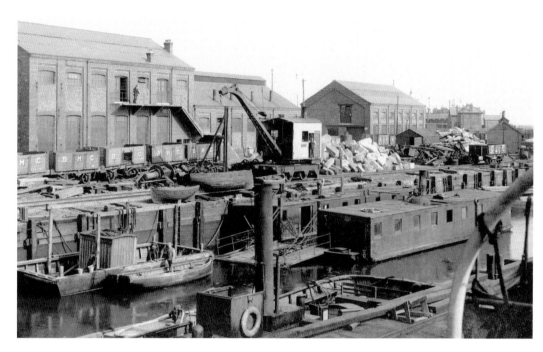

The north end of the workshops in the South Harbour, *c.* 1920. In the foreground is the old steam ferry *Jingo*, which for many years was the mid-ferry running between the Quayside and the Seven Stars. The other ferry is the spare chain ferry, which would be at the workshops for its annual overhaul. Note the Harbour Commission's own railway trucks in front of the newly built workshops.

The twin-screw steel dredger *Blyth* dredging in the upper harbour, *c.* 1910. Built in 1892 by Wm Simons & Co. Ltd of Renfrew in Scotland, the dredger was sold by Blyth Harbour Commissioners in December 1916 to Dibbles Ltd Shipbuilders, of the Belvedere Shipyard in Northam in Southampton. *Blyth* was registered at Cardiff in June 1917.

The grab barge and the dredger *Cowpen* working on the bar at the entrance to Blyth Harbour. For fifty-one years the dredger worked at Blyth; it is estimated that when she was sold to Italian owners in 1964, the *Cowpen* had removed some 20 million tons of spoil from the harbour.

A regular scene at Blyth during the Herring Season before the First World War. With Wensleydale Terrace in the background, the Scottish fisher girls are hard at work, out in all weather, gutting, washing, cleaning herring and packing them in barrels for shipment to other places. At the height of the season there would be upward of 500 girls travelling around the coast, from port to port, from northern Scotland down to Yarmouth.

THE
BLYTH HARBOUR COMMISSIONERS
GIVE NOTICE THAT A
WHITE FISH MARKET
WILL BE OPENED ON 10TH JANUARY, 1910,

in their South Harbour, and they invite owners of Fishing Vessels, Fish Buyers, and others in the trade to give the port a share of their business.

The Commissioners will afford every information and assistance to those using the port.

C. E. BALDWIN,
Clerk to the above Commissioners.

In 1910 a white fish trade was started at Blyth and by 1911 the Port of Blyth Steam Fishing Co. had been formed. Throughout that year a large fishing fleet was developed. The first five or six vessels were ex-Grimsby boats but the remainder were all newly built. With the outbreak of the First World War, the navy requisitioned many of the trawlers and Blyth became a closed port. The white fish trade did not return to Blyth after the war.

The vessel in the foreground of this picture, which was taken in approximately 1910, is the first headquarters at Blyth for the Royal Northumberland Yacht Club. This vessel had been *Robert Stephenson*, the engineer's own schooner. As the club house it was renamed *House Yacht Tyne*. The large building in the background is the Ice House, which was built in 1910.

Shortly after the First World War the old club ship *H.Y. Tyne* had to be broken up. The Yacht Club then purchased the concrete and granite built tug *Crete Hatch*, which was towed from Aberdeen and converted into a club house at Blyth, becoming *H.Y. Tyne II*.

In October 1949 the *H.Y. Tyne II* capsized and sank during a violent gale. This picture taken in approximately 1951 shows the wreckage of the old club house that, having been made of concrete, took many years to clear away. In 1952 the present *H.Y. Tyne III* was bought. This had been the ex-Calshot Spit Light Vessel No.50.

In the early 1930s the RNYC took over some of the land and buildings at the South Harbour that had been used by Cuthbert Ritson the boat builder. Here they stored their smaller craft over the winter until the outbreak of war in 1939.

Blyth Upper Harbour, c. 1963. This picture shows Bates' Loading Point and Ritson's Jetty with the chain ferry in the foreground and open country away to the north-west. On the north side of the river you have the busy ship-breaking yard of Hughes Bolckow.

Definitely not a smokeless zone, the high ferry gets steam up to cross the river once more. This vehicle ferry stopped running after the Kitty Brewster Road Bridge was opened in 1961. The *Hudson Forth*, lying at Ritson's jetty, gets steam up ready to move along to Bates' Loading Point to take on another cargo of coal. For many years Hudson vessels were regular traders out of Blyth.

In 1939 an air-sea rescue base was established in the South Harbour at Blyth. As well as being rescue boats, the high-speed wooden launches were sometimes used for towing targets so that aircraft from RAF Acklington could get target practice.

While taking on petrol at the east side of the middle jetty on the 20 May 1950, HSL 2555 suddenly exploded and became a total wreck. With the assistance of a fishing boat she was towed and beached at the south end of the Ice House. Fortunately there were no casualties.

The *Empress of Scotland* on fire at Hughes Bolckow's battleship wharf in December 1930. As can be seen the vessel is starting to list away from the quay because of the amount of water that had been pumped onto the vessel. It was four days before the fire was finally put out.

To help fight the fire on the *Empress of Scotland* tugs with fire-fighting equipment attacked the blaze from the river while firemen from all over the area fought the blaze from the quayside. The picture shows the Durham and Northumberland Collieries Fire and Rescue's appliance and Blyth's own fire engine well down the ferry slipway pumping water to the firemen in the ship-breaker's yard.

HMS *Campania* arriving at Blyth for scrapping on 11 November 1955. Built as an escort carrier in 1943 by Harland & Wolff of Belfast, she was loaned to the Festival of Britain organization in 1950 as a mobile exhibition ship. She carried the equipment for the atom bomb trials at the Monte Bello Islands near Western Australia on 3 October 1952, after which she was laid up and later sold for scrap to Hughes Bolckow of North Blyth.

Above: The launch of the 12,549 ton motor-tanker *Plumleaf* took place on Tuesday 29 March 1959, built to order for Wm Cory & Son Ltd of London. For the whole of the working life of the vessel she was chartered to the Ministry of Defence (Navy) as a Royal Fleet Auxiliary tanker.

Left: The launch party climb the stairs to the bows of the 23,000 ton bulk-ore carrier *Chapel River* towering high over Regent Street on Friday afternoon on 18 May 1962. When she entered the river she became the largest vessel to be built at Blyth. She was the same size as the *Pacific Princess*, which was built two years later.

The last shipwrights to work at Blyth shipyard were photographed in front of the last vessel, the *Rogate*, to be built by the Blyth Dry Docks & Shipbuilding Co. Ltd on 24 November 1966. From left to right, the men are, front row: Bill Coulthard, John Winters, Thomas Shields, Charles Teasdale, Ossie McCullen, Jimmy Nuttall and George Shields. Middle row: Billy Mann, Thomas Raffle, John Wilson, Jack Bates, Bob Courtney, John Young, Bill Hart and Dennis O'Brian. Back row: Ken Woods, Billy Baldwin and George Webb.

Cowpen 'B' Pit, also known as Cowpen North Pit, was renamed Bates' Pit in 1932. This picture shows the pit before the old coal washer plant was demolished in February 1961. To the right of the shaft headgear is the creeper that took the full tubs of coal up to the coal cleaning plant.

Bates' Pit No.3 shaft nearing completion in the late 1950s. Only three of the four fillers in the foreground of the picture have been identified. They are, left to right: -?-, Jimmy Quinn (at the back), Bobby Fuller and J. Rutherford.

Hennessy (Hency) Hall talking to Oliver (Ollie) Vose, the driver of the underground locomotive at the fourth north loader at Bates Pit. Note the size of the much larger coal trucks used underground at that time in modernised collieries.

Bumpers and drawers ready to leave Bates' shaft landing. The following men on the man rider trucks have been identified as, back row: W. Rumsby and H. Penn. Front row: J. White, S. White, R. Fuller, N. Aitcheson, -?-, W. Coxon, J. Strong and W. Simper. The locomotive driver is Ollie Vose.

The modernised surface plant and headgear at Bates' Pit, c. 1970. The 0-6-0 Saddle Tank steam locomotive was a common sight shunting trucks around in pit yards at most of the collieries in the north-east coal fields.

Not looking quite as cheerful as usual at the end of a shift underground, this group of men have just finished their last shift underground at Bates' Pit. Coal had been mined on this site for more than 100 years but it all came to an end on Saturday 31 May 1986 when Bates' Pit closed down.

Crofton Mill Pit, so called because it was on the site of Davison's Mill at Crofton. Work started on sinking the shaft on 26 January 1885 by the Cowpen & North Seaton Coal Co. The shaft was sunk to a depth of 558ft.

This view of the Mill Pit shows the creeper that brought the full tubs of coal from the shaft to the screens and returned the empties back to the shaft to go down the pit again to be refilled. The Mill Pit had only one shaft but its underground workings were linked to Cowpen North Pit (renamed Bates Pit in 1932) and the Isabella Pit, so either of these could be used in an emergency.

This picture shows the tippler on the screens just about to empty a full tub of coal onto the shakers that graded the coal into different sizes. The coal then passed along the picking belts where stones and other foreign matter were removed from the belt.

Crofton Mill Pit just after production ceased on Friday 18 July 1969. At its peak the annual output of the pit reached 366,000 tons with a maximum of 952 men being employed at the colliery. Some of the buildings around the shaft area still survive having been used as foundry and other engineering works.

A group of Cambois miners waiting to go underground, *c.* 1890. At its peak Cambois Pit produced 416,286 tons of coal a year, employing 1,250 men. Throughout its working life of just over 100 years Cambois Pit worked a total of seven seams of coal.

The old timber headgear at Cambois Pit and the old sandstone steam winding house beside the shaft, *c.* 1932. This shaft was sunk during the first half of the 1860s and being so close to the sea the entire sinking operations suffered water problems. The closure of Cambois Colliery came on Monday 22 April 1968.

Isabella pit, *c.* 1930. This picture shows the big chimney for the steam winding and pumping equipment at the colliery. The view of the end of the row of houses clearly shows the different heights between the front and back of the houses. The Isabella Pit ceased production of coal on Saturday 12 February 1966.

New Delaval Pit, *c.* 1927. This picture shows the headgear for the Foster and Richard shafts with the coal-screening plant between them. On Saturday 2 April 1955 the NCB announced the closure of New Delaval Colliery; the men were to be moved to other pits in the Hartley Group.

This scene was repeated in practically every mining village during the miners' strike of 1926. The soup kitchens were set up to make sure the children got at least one good meal a day. Money or foodstuff was donated by local businessmen to help keep the kitchens going.

The last tenants living at Cowpen Colliery were William Sanderson and his young wife Francis with their twenty-month-old son who lived in West Row. During February 1961 they moved into a prefabricated house at Fallow Park Avenue at Isabella Colliery.

When the full trucks of coal arrived on the staithes it was the job of the teamers to bring the full trucks over the spouts that were loading into the vessels below. The man with the wood mallet would knock out the pins that would allow the bottom boards to drop so that the coal fell down the spouts into the ship's hold.

A group of Blyth trimmers, *c.* 1920. Once the coal was in the hold of the ship it was the job of the trimmers to make sure that the coal was evenly spread within the hold of the vessel. Note the unusual shape of the shovels used by the trimmers; this was so that the men could kneel and sweep the coal with their shovel into the corners or any other awkward places.

The unveiling of the Boer War Memorial took place on Wednesday 22 July 1903 in front of the old post office at the head of Bridge Street. The memorial stood here until the late 1950s when it was moved to its present site at Ridley Park.

On Saturday 19 July 1919, Blyth celebrated peace and victory at the end of the First World War with a day of general rejoicing. Blyth council constructed an imposing Triumphal Arch in the Market Place, which thousands of local people came to admire.

Many of the shop and other business premises in the town were a glory of colour and decorations. Both of the town's railway bridges were decorated as victory arches. This picture shows the railway bridge beside the station (now Safeway). The other railway bridge was beside Ridley Park.

During Saturday afternoon there was a procession around the town ending at Croft Park. This picture shows the children marching up Waterloo Road. At ten o'clock at night there was a torchlight procession to Ridley Park where there was a fine firework display.

During Blyth's peace celebrations at the end of the First World War, Hedley's Fountain in front of the Central Hall at the Market Place was used as a temporary memorial to the men of Blyth who had not returned from the war.

This 1920s picture shows the members of the Blyth Salvation Army in front of their citadel in the market place. The Salvation Army hall was gutted by fire on Friday 24 March 1933 and later Woolworths was built on the site.

Left: From 1925 until the Blyth carnivals ended in 1938 there was a Carnival King and Queen (both parts being played by men) and a court jester. In this picture the court jester is Jimmy Luke who played this role from 1934 to 1938. From 1934 to 1936 the King was Bob Simpson and the Queen was Norman Robson. In 1937 and 1938 the King was Storey Cully and the Queen was George Cantley.

Below: This picture shows the procession of the first carnival coming down Regent Street on Wednesday 3 September 1924. The parade was led by the band of the 72nd Brigade Royal Field Artillery (TA) followed by Blyth's new fire engine. This was followed by the schools' tableaux performed by school children from Standard III upwards. In all there were seventeen different groups and four bands in the procession.

Even throughout the depression years of the 1920s and 1930s the Blyth Carnival continued until the threat of war brought them to an end in 1938. This picture shows the carnival procession being led by Cowpen Colliery Brass Band down Regent Street on Wednesday 4 September 1929.

Each year in the Carnival there was a small prize given for the best local tradesman's advertising tableaux. This prize was won more than once by George Armstrong, the fruit and potato merchant of Regent Street, for his decorated motor wagon.

Throughout the years of Blyth Carnival there were always a number of prizes for the best-groomed horse with tableaux, best-decorated horses and vehicles, and the best-groomed horses on their own. Most years Blyth Co-operative Society had horses taking part in the carnival.

Left: George 'Pie' Smith took part in many of the Blyth Carnivals until his death in 1935. He was the Carnival Queen in 1929 and 1930 along with Ted Warner as the King and Bob Simpson as the court jester. This picture shows him in fancy dress, enjoying himself in a dog cart that looks too small for him.

Opposite above: Ronnie McCall enjoying a spin around the streets of Blyth. Twenty-one-year-old Ronnie, a display supervisor for Blyth Co-operative Society, looks remarkably confident on this Penny Farthing bicycle. His ride was part of the Society's centenary celebrations on Saturday 30 June 1964.

Opposite below: A regular character around Blyth in the middle of the twentieth century was Mr Joseph Martino, seen here on 26 January 1964 with his roast chestnut barrow. In the summer time he would be seen around the town with his ice cream barrow.

Men of the Blyth Shipyard Home Guard in approximately 1940 with their First World War water-cooled machine guns. The men, left to right, are: Sgt Edmond Sadd, Hedley Sanderson, 'Badger' Harrison, ?, Sid Brown (joiner), George Carr and Ralph Bird.

The last parade of the Blyth detachment of the town's ARP (Air Raid Precautions) seen passing along Regent Street at the end of the war in 1945. After this date they where known as the Civil Defence, a volunteer organisation which continued in force until the late 1960s.

This picture shows one of the tile shed cottages, *c.* 1880. To the south of Wensleydale Terrace was the Tile & Patent Marble Works. Richard Wilson is listed as the owner of these works during the first quarter of the nineteenth century. The patent marble was really only glazed bricks.

Listed in the 1881 census as Croft Tower, this building stood on the site of where the Tower Garage now stands in Regent Street. In the early1900s the property was used as a common lodging house. For about twenty years from the 1930s it was the Tower Crisp Factory until it was demolished.

The church of St Mary in Horton stands high and proud on a ridge when viewed from the east. It had been built in 1827 on the site of a very ancient chapel. About a mile to the south-east was the site of Horton Castle and somewhere between the two may well have been the lost medieval village of Horton.

Blyth Chapel of Ease, built in 1751, was plain on the inside with a gallery at the western end. In the mid-nineteenth century the music to sing by was provided by a hand-cranked barrel organ with three barrels and ten tunes to a barrel. When St Cuthbert's church opened in 1885 the old chapel became the church hall.

In its latter years this building was known as the New Delaval Independent Methodist Church, although it was initially used as a Christian Lay Church in 1883 before being rebuilt in 1902. Rising like a phoenix from the ashes the church was rebuilt again after having been badly damaged by fire on New Year's Eve in 1970.

For a number of years after the small mining village of South Newsham had disappeared, the little Methodist chapel stood all on its own by the roadside as if waiting for someone to find a use for the building.

St Cuthbert's ladies sewing circle in approximately 1915 in the vicarage garden in Northumberland Street. In the front row are: Miss T. Dinsdale, Miss McFarlane, Miss Bennett and ? Packnoham. Middle row: Miss Warwick, Mrs Dixon, Miss Dinsdale, Miss Kelsey, Mrs Scott, Miss Robinson and Mrs Ryan. Back row: Miss Atkins, Mrs Shy, M. Schofield, Revd Hutchins, Mrs Newstead, Mrs Watts, Mrs Schofield, Miss Percy and Mrs Marley.

Children of the Ballast Hill Sunday School in approximately 1890 waiting to go on a Sunday School outing. By the early 1900s this building had become the Norwegian church for Scandinavian seamen in the port.

Right: The bronze bust in memory of Viscount Matthew White Ridley who gave the land for a public park. The bust was carved by George Skee, a local sculptor, and was erected in 1909 near the entrance to Ridley Park.

Below: Ridley Park Lodge was built 1903 as the 14 acres of land given by Lord Ridley were being laid out with trees, flower beds and ornamental walks; tennis courts and bowling greens were also provided. There was a fine bandstand where on summer evenings concerts would be given by colliery and military brass bands as well as other entertainers.

During the summer season of 1905 Messrs George and Edwards White Coons provided nightly entertainment from 14 June until the end of September in Ridley Park, weather permitting, or at the Alexandra Hall on wet nights. This Edwardian music hall troupe seems to consist of five regulars, Messrs George and Edwards, Teddy Volbec, Bob Stephenson and Tom Bishop, with guest artists joining them each week.

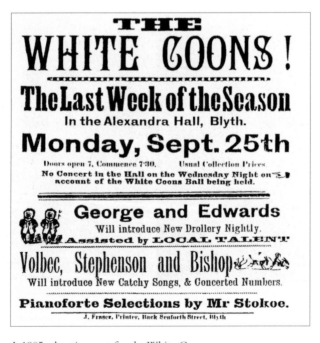

A 1905 advertisement for the White Coons.

A Newsham musical family, *c.* 1930. Three generations of the Clough family who for many years maintained the popularity of the Northumberland small pipes. The tallest figure in the back row is Fred Picknell, a skilled pipe maker who made pipes for the Cloughs. The seated gentleman was a local well-known sportsman, Mr Dan Murray.

The second Theatre Royal, built in 1900, looking sad and forlorn just before it was demolished in the mid-1970s. Over the years many well-known thespians trod the boards here before it closed in February 1959. A number of television stars started their careers with repertory companies at Blyth, such as the actor Stratford Johns and the news reader Mike Neville with Tyne Tees Television.

Richard (Dicky) Fynes, the father of live theatre at Blyth, was born at Newcastle in 1826 and died at Blyth on 16 September 1892. At the age of eight years he became a pit lad and at the age of ten he ran away to sea. After a few years he returned to coal mining. In 1865 he bought the old Octagon chapel to use as a furniture salesroom, which he later converted into a music hall, which, after a fire, he rebuilt as the larger Theatre Royal. 1873 saw the publication of his *History of the Northumberland & Durham Miners*. His favourite quote was 'It is little for many that one can do, but the many can always help one'.

Some of the members of the 3rd Blyth Scouts Troop, *c.* 1950. They are as follows from left to right, front row: William Laidler, Brian Tosson and John Gunn. Back row: John Brown, the Skipper Bill Eadington and Stan Watson.

Members of the Blyth Methodist Zion church, Troop of the Boys Brigade. The years between the First and Second World Wars was the heyday of Blyth Boys Brigade. The Boys Brigade also had a fine band that was much in demand around the town as well as at the church.

About twenty-two troops of Scouts, Rovers, Guides, Cubs and Brownies took part in the St George's Day Parade on 26 April 1962. After being inspected by the County Commissioner for Scouts, Mr A. W. Smith, on Blyth Market Place, they marched off to St Cuthbert's church via Stanley Street.

The North East's first ever fibre-glass church spire was made at Blyth by Freedman Bros Ltd, of Quay Road. The 70ft-long spire was taken by road on Monday 27 May 1963 to Cassop-cum-Quarrington, which is a few miles from Durham city where the spire was mounted on a 20ft-high iron base.

HMS *Token* tied up beside the south staithes at Blyth at the end of May 1965. At this period the submarine was being used as a training vessel for men of the Commonwealth Navies.

The Mayor of Blyth, Alderman J.R. Curry, jokes as he looks through the periscope of HMS *Token*: 'I've got the power station in my sights'. Looking on are Mr E.W. Carter the town clerk (centre) and Lt-Cmdr. M.H. Everett.

Fire Chief Fred Naisbitt proudly shows off his new fire station in Union Street. It had officially opened on 3 September 1924 after the brigade moved from the old horse station in Seaforth Street, which was too small for their needs.

It took more than thirty firemen and fire appliances from Blyth, Gosforth, Whitley Bay, Ashington and Morpeth under the command of Mr William Muir the chief fire officer to put out this blaze at Cooknell's plastics factory in Quay Road in Blyth on Tuesday 21 March 1961.

The remains of Newsham pottery kilns. The Newsham Art & Pottery Works were built by George Skee, a local sculptor, under the patronage of Lord Ridley of Blagdon in 1910. Situated near Park Farm Cottages in Newsham, the works were closed during the First World War and never really got going again after the war.

A group of folk dancers entertain a large crowd on the promenade near the beach gardens during the 1963 August Bank Holiday. For about the first twenty years after the end of the Second World War, Easter to August saw regular entertainment of all kinds held in the bandstand or on the promenade.

Ministerial consent was given to build Blyth 'A' power station in February 1955, seen here under construction. The station came on line in June 1960. During four of its first five years, the 'A' station headed the table for generating the most power in the country.

Work commenced on the construction of Blyth's 'B' power station in 1962. When the four generators, two of 275MW and two of 350MW, came on line in September 1966 the station became one of Europe's largest generating plants. Both stations burned in excess of 3 million tons of coal a year.

For those living in the Blyth and Ashington areas, the four white concrete chimneys of Blyth power station were always a sign that one was nearly home. For more than forty years they were a well-known landmark for coastal shipping, and aircraft heading for Newcastle airport.

Watched by thousands of people, the final chapter in the life of Blyth power station took place on Sunday 7 December 2003 when the last parts of the power station came crashing to the ground. It seems strange not seeing the chimneys there, looming over the town.

Above: Blyth Port Isolation Hospital was built in the mid-1890s and used by people from Blyth and Cowpen as well as seamen. There are still people in Blyth who, as children, spent time in this hospital having had scarlet fever, diphtheria or enteric fever. The hospital was destroyed during an air raid in the Second World War, but thankfully nobody was injured.

Left: Matron Clemens sitting with her dog on a seat in the grounds of the Isolation Hospital at Factory Point in Cowpen. The seat was made from driftwood taken from the River Blyth.

Ninety-one-year-old William R. Sullivan, the last of the Old Contemptibles at Blyth. He is seen here in 1985 about to lay his wreath to fellow comrades who were lost in the First World War. Bill always laid a wreath on the eleventh day of the eleventh month no matter which day of the week it was. Bill Sullivan continued this practice right up to within a year or so of his death in 1991.

Other local titles published by Tempus

Blyth
BLYTH LOCAL STUDIES GROUP

Once a small quayside town, it was not until the 'Slake' was filled in at the end of the nineteenth century that Blyth could grow alongside its industry. With the railway's closure in 1964, the shipyard's in 1967 and the end of coal working at Bates' Pit in 1986, more than 100 years of industry that had helped to shape the town of Blyth came to an end. This book charts this rise and fall.
07524 0773 2

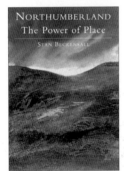

Bedlingtonshire
EVAN MARTIN

This collection of over 200 photographs covers every village in Bedlingtonshire from Netherton to Cambois and from Hartford Bridge to Sheepwash. For many centuries it was a rural area, then the ironworks came in the mid-eighteenth century, followed by coalmining 100 years later. These formed the community's industrial base and changed the face of the area. The mines and ironworks have now gone but the area's history is remembered in this volume.
07524 0784 8

Northumberland The Power of Place
STAN BECKENSALL

This book shows the outstanding natural beauty, distinctive geology and rich archaeology of this county. Famous sites that delight visitors – Berwick, Holy Island, Hadrian's Wall and the Cheviots – are featured alongside lesser-known places such as Old Berwick, Edlington, Ford and Etal. When layers of time are peeled from these special places, the result is a microcosm of the county, captured in prose and poetry, photographs from the air and ground, and paintings and drawings.
07524 1907 2

Prehistoric Northumberland
STAN BECKENSALL

For this book, Stan Beckensall's study area lies largely to the north of Hadrian's Wall, which cuts a swathe across much older sites. His account looks at how landscape was used since hunter-gatherers roamed the wilderness, through the great changes brought about by farming, the erection of monuments, burials, settlements and defences. He explains how tools, weapons, pottery and jewellery help build a picture of life in prehistoric Northumberland.
07524 2543 9

If you are interested in purchasing other books published by Tempus, or in case you have difficulty finding any Tempus books in your local bookshop, you can also place orders directly through our website
www.tempus-publishing.com